Contents

All sorts of worms

Look closely at any patch of earth in a garden or park and you will usually see a wriggly worm.

Worms that live in the soil are called earthworms. There are several sorts of earthworms.

Most earthworms are reddish-brown and are about as long as your hand.

There are many different kinds of worms around the world, and they come in many colours and sizes. Some are so tiny that they are hard to see. Others, such as the Giant Earthworm of Australia, grow up to 4 metres long!

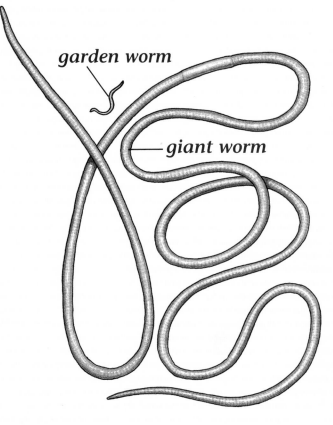

This giant worm from Australia is no wider than your finger but is as long as a car! Compare its length to that of the garden worm.

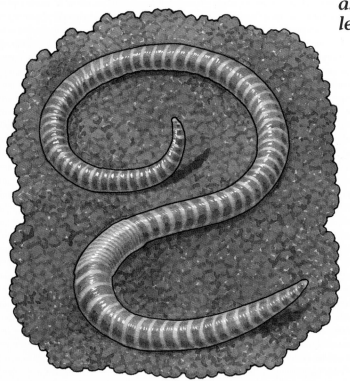

◀ The brandling has a stripy coat. This makes it is easy to recognize, unlike most other kinds of earthworm.

Finding earthworms

Earthworms live in damp soil where there are bits of dead plants to eat. Most of them live near the top of the soil – about one spade's depth under the ground.

Earthworms are easy to find if you know where to look. Dig the garden with a spade or fork and you are sure to find some in the soil.

Earthworms live in woods, meadows and gardens, especially under lawns, and among the damp, dead leaves under hedges and trees. Worms love compost heaps, and you often see them wriggling through the mush.

There are very few worms in sandy soil. This is because rainwater drains away quickly and the soil becomes too dry for them.

A worm's body

A worm is a very simple animal. It has no skeleton, no lungs, no eyes or ears. Its body is a wriggly tube made of many tiny segments. Each one is filled with liquid and has bristles that help the worm move.

Front

Mouth

Segment

Bristles

Saddle
(where a worm's eggs are made)

Back

Worms can tell the difference between light and dark. Whenever you uncover a worm, it tries to get back in the dark.

Earthworms breathe through their skins, taking in air that is trapped in the soil.

On wet days these air pockets fill with water, and worms have to shoot up to the surface. If they didn't, they would drown underground.

A worm's body is damp but not slimy. Its front end is more pointed than the back.

Feeding

Earthworms feed on the rotting parts of dead plants. They have no teeth or jaws, so the food they eat must be very soft. Sometimes they nibble it with their tiny lips, but usually they just suck it up.

◄ Worms also feed on soil. They take in any goodness as it works through their body, then get rid of any waste in a worm cast.

In the daytime, worms usually stay under the soil, feeding on the roots of dead plants. At night, when it is dark and damp, they crawl up to the surface and search for dead leaves, which they then drag under the ground.

A pile of dead leaves is a favourite feeding place for worms. Sometimes they store the leaves in their tunnels until they rot. This helps to make a good soil.

Moving

Worms have strong muscles to help them move. There are ring-shaped muscles inside each segment, which make their body shrink or spread out. Other muscles run along their body, and make it grow short or long.

A worm's damp body helps it to move easily through the soil.

A worm's bristles are very important in helping it to move. The creature digs its bristles into the soil to anchor itself.

1 *A worm moves by pointing its head in the direction it wants to go. It anchors the back of its body, and the head end becomes thicker.*

2 *It then stretches its body to push through the soil. It anchors the front of its body and brings up the rear.*

Tunnelling

A worm makes tunnels partly by pushing its way between the soil and partly by eating it. As the worm moves forward, its body coats the walls with slime. This makes the tunnels stronger but, even so, they soon collapse.

A worm tunnelling its way through the soil.

Worm tunnels make airy spaces under the soil, and help rainwater drain away. The soil becomes looser and finer, making it easier for plants to grow.

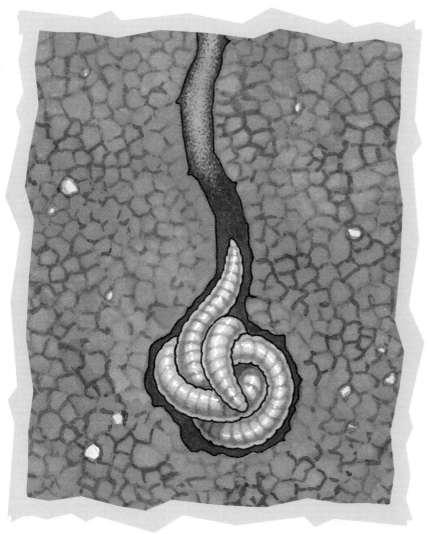

Some worms burrow deeper underground when the weather is too cold or too dry. They push down to about a metre below the surface, then coil up and go to sleep. They wake when the weather improves.

This worm is sleeping through a hot, dry summer in a burrow deep underground.

Mating

Worms like to mate on a warm, damp night. The two worms lie next to one another, and wrap themselves together with slime. They stay close like this for several hours.

After mating, the saddle on each worm makes a sticky belt of slime. The worm wriggles out of its belt and lays its eggs in it. The belt then seals up and makes a hard cocoon. It is about 3 mm long.

A close up of the saddle, where the eggs are made. A worm must mate with another worm to make eggs. Every worm has both male and female parts to its body, so any worm it meets can be a mate.

Hatching

Worms' eggs take several weeks or months to grow in the cocoon. In that time, some of the eggs will die. Often just one or two worms hatch out of the cocoon.

A worm's cocoon.

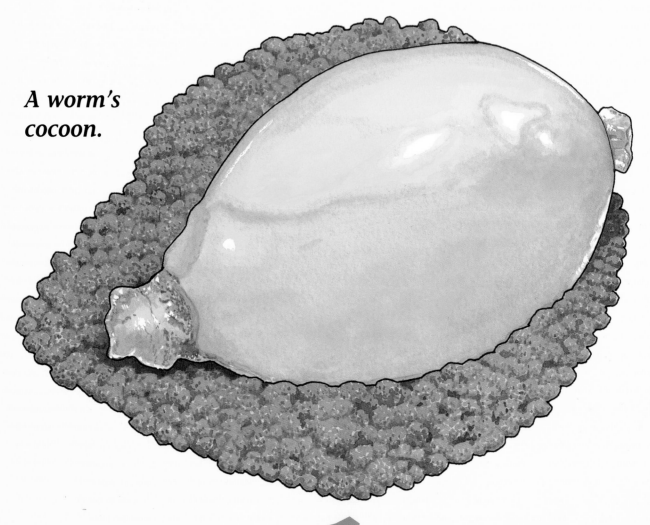

Young earthworms are about as long as your thumbnail. They are whiter than their parents, and have no saddles at first, but otherwise they look just the same.

▲

Adult worm with young worms.

It takes 18 months for a young worm to grow up and lay eggs of its own. If it can avoid being eaten, the worm may live in the soil for ten years or more.

Enemies

Worms have many enemies such as hedgehogs and shrews. Both of these animals are active at night when worms come out to feed.

A mole is an earthworm's greatest enemy. It may eat 25 worms a day as it tunnels under the ground. If it catches more worms than this, it stores them in a special pantry.

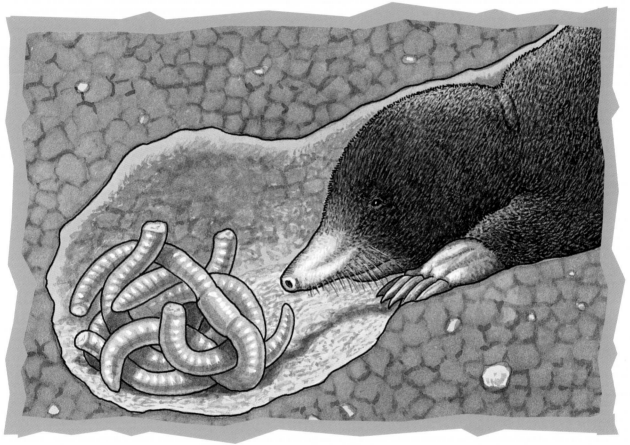

A mole's pantry full of worms.

Moles stop worms escaping from their pantry by biting off their heads. This does not kill the worm. In time, its head grows again and the worm may be able to escape!

Food for birds

Some birds eat worms. Blackbirds, thrushes and starlings all visit gardens and parks, looking and listening for the tiny movements that earthworms make in the ground.

When a bird spots a worm it grabs it by the tail, but may have a hard job pulling it out. The worm anchors itself in the ground with its bristles, and pulls back hard with its powerful muscles.

A tussle between a bird and worm is just like a tug-of-war.

Birds hunt for worms in spring when other food is scarce. But as fruits ripen in summer and autumn, birds usually leave worms alone.

Worm wonders!

There are over 1800 different kinds of worms around the world.

A medium-sized garden probably contains about 20,000 earthworms.

A worm's body is made up of about 250 segments.

A famous scientist called Charles Darwin believed that the worm was the world's most important animal because it encourages plants to grow.

Without worms, the soil would be wet, heavy and hard to work.

Worms eat about one-third of their body weight every day. That's like you eating 20 loaves of bread!

Every crumb of soil in parks and gardens has passed through the body of a worm.

Worm casts are very good for the garden. The soil in them is very fine and contains valuable food from plants.

Earthworm farms sell worms to gardeners to help them improve their soil.

Many fish enjoy a juicy worm. That's why fishermen use worms as bait.

Worms have blood but no heart.

Glossary

Bristle   A tiny, stiff hair.

Cocoon   The hard, oval case in which a worm's eggs grow.

Compost heap   A place where people pile dead plants, and fruit and vegetable peelings. These rot down into compost, which can be used to feed the soil.

Muscle   The part of an animal's body that helps it to move.

Saddle   The swollen part of an adult worm's body where the eggs are made, and which it uses during mating to make a cocoon.

Shrew   A small, wild animal, rather like a mouse, but with a longer nose.

Worm cast   The soil that passes out of a worm's body and forms a little pile on the grass.

Index

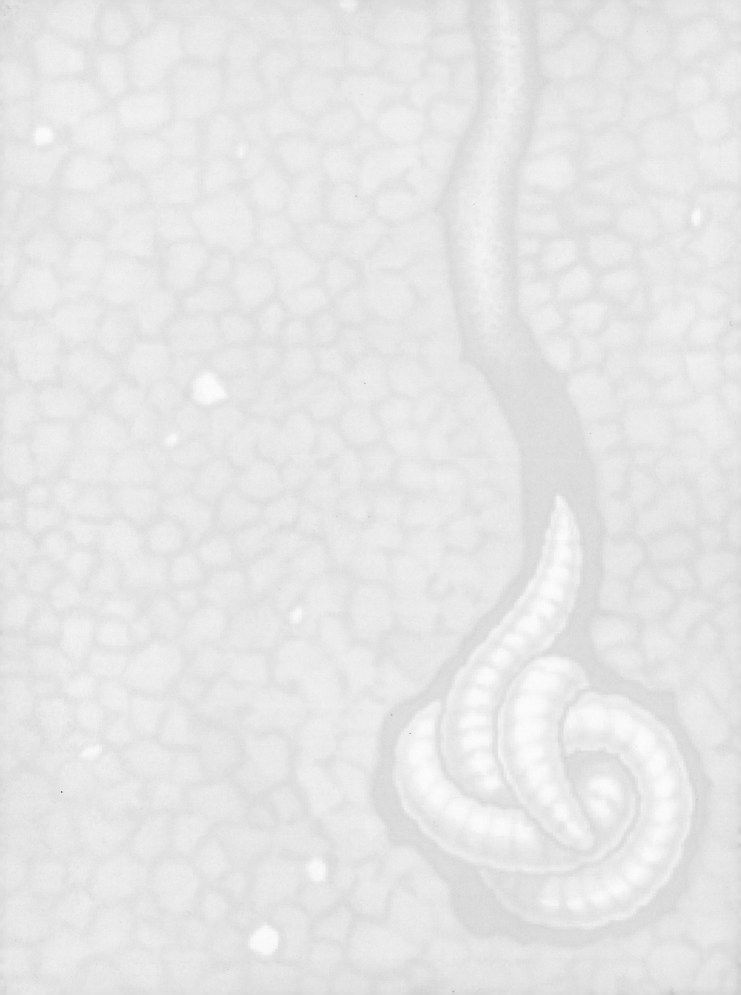